Sy

To Ann,
With much love
Jan. P. 95/96.

# ALL HALLOWS

## Symphony in Three Movements

A Poem

by

Tony Conran

GOMER

*First Impression—October 1995*

ISBN 1 85902 273 1

This volume is published with the support
of the Arts Council of Wales

Printed in Wales at
Gomer Press, Llandysul, Dyfed

# ACKNOWLEDGEMENTS

'Investiture 1969' appeared in *Radical Wales* and two short sequences, 'Maps, for Paul and Verena's Wedding' and 'Soldier', in *The New Welsh Review*. The first section of 'All Hallows' was read at Paul Davies's funeral in Bangor Cathedral and later published in *Poetry Wales*.

The 'Soldier' sequence was originally commissioned for an inter-religious Christmas service during the Gulf War, with both Kuwaitis and Iraqis present. I was haunted by the shattered columns of the Iraqi army on the way out of Kuwait, iron graveyards across the desert. The titles of the individual sections were added when I decided to include the sequence, along with 'Investiture', as the central movement of the symphony.

# ONE

## THE SHADOW

### Notations for Raymond Garlick

You must come—start this pilgrimage
Can you come?—send an ode or elegy
In the old way and raise our heritage.

'Poem from Llanybri' (Lynette Roberts)

a stupendous aborting of the green force
within us . . ..

. . . no day like this
for seven hundred years.

'A Diary for St David's Week, 1979'
(Ianws—Jon Dressel)

## COLLECTED POEMS

'Here's your copy,' you said.
Lettered in the out tray
Like a sampler of angels—

Forty years of you.  Eric Gill's
Alphabet demurely hinting
The tinted words.

Forty years.  From the Third Door
On Aber Henfelin, the holms
And ynysoedd, the salt spaces

Where the journey begins,
Penfro, with its mixed blessing          *Pembroke Dock*
Of the prophesied King:                  *Henry Tudor*

Under the great Keep
The cry and shrivel
Of kinship under the stars.

To a place of rock, the grey
Llechi of the Fronts,                    *Blaenau Ffestiniog*
The rain-white lichened world.

The waste in the chittering slates,
In the God, in the people
Eroding to scree,

In the land, in the language—
That quirky demoralised
Scree-sense of survival,

In the rough stuff of the quarries
Against the exploitative
And the kind.  Waste—

8

And the wonder of it, trove
Of its antique richness—
Drove you at last to easier

Less compromising
Strangeness. The Netherlands
Gave you at least

The strict status of aliens.
Happiness was embossed
On the finity of the known.

For the family, exile was green,
Was Europe. But the babe
Tumbles to manhood, the breast

Buds, the secret hairs
Trumpet: hiraeth
Of land answered, deep to deep . . .

Forty years. 'They've done a lovely job on it,'
I said, and later
Read it through at a sitting—

Like finding old family china,
Cups you remember by, plates
Never so ordering since

Of the things to be loved—
Discovering new meanings
Like new stars in the Plough.

# CHOICES

But all that was secondary—
The heart's foyer to where
You did not choose.

O yes, Raymond, you came back,
And that was choice.
You chose your moment.

The dragons were limping                  *Welsh language*
Into the air. With the dawn                    *struggles*
They went out.

Young men, girls. In the streets,
In the white moorlands
They went out. They sat down.

Teachers, old men. They were bridges
For their people.
They stretched out. They sang.

You chose your moment.
The sword of peace, the huge armour
Of Gandhi's cloak.

They sat down                              *Canonization of*
To consider the matter. To sing.            *16th cent. Welsh*
In Rome. In Abertawe.                       *Catholic martyrs*

There were things you did not choose,
But the secondary matters,
The martyrdom acclaimed, you chose.

## SANCTITY

The martyrdom of the Saints
Made them human.
Humanity flowered in their death
Like the smoke from a pipe.

The soft textured roundedness
Of simple folk—
You learnt it
In a finger's touch, a rosary.

Even then, Rome's
Acclamation was foreign to you,
Its colours too heraldic
For the peace you touched.

Your fingers prickled.
Embers singed them.
You learnt martyrdom
Like domestic science.

You stitched a shirt for us.
You set before us a meal.

## PROLOGUE IN HEAVEN

Now there was a day when the Sensations
Infolded,

      When the Intuitions
Darted like fishes in the shining
Mirror,

      When the Feelings
Gathered on the desireless needle—

When the Thoughts lay still as
Blackberries under the hedge.

It was a day and it was a night.

And likewise, the Shadow
Insinuated himself.
'Should I not also be
In this fishbowl,
This bramble bush?' said
The Shadow.

'Ho,' said Imagination,
'Where have you come?'

It was starry, it was mist.

'Going to and fro in the earth,'
The Shadow said,
'Walking up and down upon it.'

'Ho, Shadow,' said
Imagination,
'Have you observed my creature Raymond?
How he bears himself—'

(It was a shining glass, it was adversity)

12

'He is coming to my festival
He carries the sponge of vinegar
To give me. He lays his goat foot
Gingerly among the privates.
He will play me aboard
Like a bosun.
He fingers his flute.
He will judge like a poet.'

'Want to bet?' said
The Shadow?

                And the Indignations
Crowded into the forecourt to hear him.
He dragged out a sack.

'Not I,' said Imagination.

                But nevertheless
Like Efnisien at the feast
The Shadow squeezed it, played
Badger in the bag,
Until skulls broke,
Eyeballs were bursting,
Tongues torn out.

'Play your pipe now,' he smiled,
'Pipe me aboard.'

And in the single red darkness of the time
The Shadow climbed upon the Cross
Like a lantern.

## BUS STOP

Opposite where one stood
In the intensity of waiting
Before hospital visits


A wall looked at.
A wall not seen.


A child whose orbits in the whirling of death
Narrowed
To the stone.


A wall describing pain.
In the petrified astonishment
Comfortless.


Your child so sick was like a slime over the sun.
Like a polluted sea that will not breathe.
Like a gaschamber filling with silence.


Your imagination
Immaculate.
A wall looked at.


A wall not seen.

# OFFERING

Two in every three
Were dead in Rama,
But you woke happy.
The child of your loins would live.


Into the body of mortality
A wound like a circumcision
Took you to the temple.


The Reciprocities received you.
You offered
The two doves, or two young pigeons


Usual
For a manchild,
For a purity.


The birds of Venus danced and cooed to each other,
Bowed and hummed and honoured their partners
With fluffed-up wings, for the blood of Isaac . . .

## HOMERS

To the Shadow hanging on the cross
The two doves fluttered.
They lighted on his shoulders—
Odin's crows
Whispering in his ear.


They were telling him
The loves of the world,
The braveries—
Shuffling their feathers
In the excitement of it.


Did you tell them that, Raymond?
Did you throw them to the wind
Saying
'Go out, pigeons bach—'
Did you?

# HEROES

'Poets of the world
Judge the brave.' Did he say
Judge? That severe man
At the rock, the cashel
Of the Otadini,

Embro, Auld Reekie,
Caer Eidin—as they drank
The blue mead, as they
Jostled for the tidbits
—This young warrior and that—

Along the barbecues, men
Turning the spits
With the touch of mechanics,
The far-sighted charisma
Of men doing women's work—

The ritual speech
Of Hell's Angels
Out on a binge,
Commandoes in the sobering
Proximity of meat.

(Jessed peregrines strutted
Round the hearths, scuttered
Like hens, and the bitches
Nuzzled the palm, growled
For the oozing bone . . .)

Food for the crows
At Catterick, the eagles
Grey-hatted over
Yorkshire streams,
The timid wolves.

Did Aneirin tell you
'Judge'?   You
Whose vegetarian gut
Hardly (you told me
Over my meat Ceylon)

Could contemplate
The ingestion of a prawn?
But indeed, the young men
Were walking into battle,
Into no man's land
.

Walking in the grey
Morning, brave
For us to judge
The white of Gandhi's dhoti,
The loins of peace.

# OVER THE TOP

Across the gathered churches—
Barbed wire
Like brown archipelagos—
Across the pitiful ditches
Of sobriety—


Across the minefields
Of good families—
Across the interior
Of wayward snipers—
Across bluffs . . .


Each precious unwrapping
Of the good sword,
The conscience saved
From rust—
Each bayonet.


Stepping it out—
Tumbling companies
In the hollow morning
Gathered
Like the bottom of a scree.

# HIS FAMILY ARRESTED

Precise dreamer, you were melded
To the allegories.
You were Long Will in the Land.


It was you dozing in the garden.
You heard the clatter of iron,
The politeness of menace.


Suddenly you were Peter.
You were prized into court.
You were drift.


Hustlers of justice.
Pert and insolent Pilate.
The cock crowing.


Poets of the world judge
The brave. Son, wife, sister
To Jerusalem to joust.


Long Will, hobbler of dreams,
Watching through the window of sleep
As they counted the nails.


'My hope is on what is to come.'

## BILL OF LADING

Specification.  Country 133.
WALES / CYMRU.  Oaks
On the quickening hillside
Sprouting.


Stag, owl and salmon
Reservists.  Daffodil
Through the woodland
Sounding.


The two crisp languages
Pulling like sails
Our barge
Into open sea.


We had a future.  Bilingual
Wales, a destination
And a tide
Turning.

## ALL THE FUN OF THE FAIR

Lightly, like a conjuror,
With the flip concentration
Of a fairground,
The shadow unpinned itself
From the cross.


It winked at us—
'Ho, boyos,' it said,
'What's in it for me?'


(And the doves giggled like schoolgirls)


Oxford voices
Keep out.
King and his counting house
Keep out.
All the soldiers on parade
Keep out.


'Oo, there's lovely,' said the doves.


'Oh, yes,' said the Shadow,
'It's been a good party.
But what's it to me?'


On the thirteenth day of Christmas
(Gŵyl Ddewi Sant)
Two turtle doves
Flew away over
The mulberry tree.

## CURRICULUM VITAE

'Mister to most, a formal man'—
You notated enthusiasms,
A kind, principled outsider
In Wales, gradually
Rooting in the green and white
Peace that you wanted.  Teacher
Of peace, you hobbled
In dignified calm
To literature.  Towards
Wales, towards
Europe, towards
Rome.  In the low low lands
Of Holland you built you
A boat, you built you
A replica of a tall
Ship, a Dutch brig
For the adventures of peace.

A Dutch brig
Called Wales.  It was floating
—Look!—in the green and white
Peace.  With four and twenty
Sailor-lads you could
Box it about the main.

What tethered it?
What stopped the tall
Dutch brig of Wales
From sailing in the timeless sea?

—How do you like it, sir?  Castles?
County Schools?  Referendum?

From sailing in the lowlands low . . .

# REFERENDUM

It was a day and it was a night.

In Llansteffan, never such a day
For seven hundred years.

Ianws the Yank, Raymond Cymro-Sais,
Cowered in history. The times
Flowed past like sheep.

Ó Conaráin in Arfon cowered.
'Keep you head down, boy,'
Said Gruffydd the beak's son.
'I've been here before.'

'Five hundred years . . .' said Owain in Sycharth.

'A green force aborted,' said Ianws to Raymond.

'Ten years of boredom,' says Tripp in Caerdydd.

## BELLE VIEW

And I watched outside the Belle View in Bangor
That night.  The fairground in the A5,
Cars slowing for the tipsy crowdlets
Welling up from the College roads.  I saw
John Dwy-Geiniog dance like a young goat
With a Union Jack on his shoulders.  I saw
Cyril Halfpint climb through the rhetoric of ale
To the Four Branches of his joy.  I saw
Englishmen already slipping the leash
Of what interest they had.  I saw
The Blaid apologetic
For a nation foreclosed.

## THE TREE

And likewise a wounded beast
With wings that gulped the air, the Shadow
Dragged itself from the badlands.


'Ho,' said Imagination
Like the Mariner drinking his blood to speak,
'Where have you come?'


'Going to and fro in the earth,'
The Shadow said,
'Walking up and down upon it.'


'Shadow,' said Imagination,
'What of my creature Raymond?
Does he ride the storm like Pity,
Like a naked new-born babe? —'


(It was desert, it was dead bones)


'Is he coming to my festival?
I am thirsty. Has he the milk
Of his mother-wit to bring me?'


'He is coming,' said the Shadow.


'I am loud with pain. Has he the flute
Of his silence to soothe me?
Will he heal me like a poet?'


(It was blast, it was whitsun)


In the dull red of the fires

'Look,' said the Shadow,
'That withered tree.  It moves
Towards us, and the lips on its branches
Cry of dishonour, like a grey defilement
Over the land.'


       'Is that my creature?
I am listening,' said Imagination.
'Let him play!'

# TWO

## SOLDIER

( A Christmas scherzo )

and

## INVESTITURE

( Trio )

# THE SOLDIER

## (Part 1)

### SHOPPING

I am worth what others suffer for me.
The currency is pain. In the Ice Age
I first heard the jingle of it.
People against bear, against wolf, against people.

In the hosting millions of me
I am the limits of wealth.
Sooner or later, power cannot suffer enough.

## PRESENT

Most places in the world
I am luxury goods.
The suffering I cost
Is simple as Christmas.

I am unwrapped at parades.
The Good Fairy
Takes the salute—

Rachel in Ephrath crying,
The mother of us
Weeping in Ramah
Because her children are not.

## STOCKING

In every man, male of the species,
A soldier is wrapped.

Just as, in every baby
There is a corpse.

Just as, in every beggarman
The Redeemer of the world.

# INVESTITURE, 1969

## (Trio)

*La connais-tu, Dafné, cette ancienne romance . . .*

Gérard de Nerval


The old tear-jerker, do you know it, Cymru,
At shattered root or under churchyard yew,
In unmade roads, or weedy in public gardens,
The sobstuff that always sprouts up new?


Towers do you recognise, and the Golden Gate,
And the sour fruit printed by your teeth,
And the deep cave, not open to visitors,
Where the drunk, beaten dragon-seed sleep?


The gods, they've come back!  London's pretty boy
Virginal and neat, fresh as a frilled lettuce,
Kneels to his Dam!  World shudders with prophecy!


O raddled Britannia still sucking her dream!
O fort of Constantine, functional yet!
Ah, the police!  Ah, benevolent military!


33

# THE SOLDIER

## (Part 2)

### PARTY GAMES

Rich man, you've got some pain to buy me?
Poor man, give me that pain.
Beggarman, I am you by myself.
Thief, honour me.


Rich man, it's justice is it?
Poor man, leave it.
Beggarman, I am homeless under the night.
Thief, I am loot.

## DRESSING UP

In every wardrobe there is a soldier
Mothballed in the corner.
Don't fool yourself, friend.


We can only die once.

# BOXING DAY

Right. Left. Right. Left.
Left. Left. Left.


The snuff. The desert sand.
Vultures strutting like Generals


Baldheaded.


Left. Left. Left.

# THREE

## ALL HALLOWS

A Wassail for Paul Davies

Sculptor, painter, earth-mover and
teacher

died All Hallows, 1993

and for Verena, his widow

The Mari Lwyd (grey or holy Mary or Mare) is a horse's skull in a
cloak, taken from house to house in South Wales, a Christmas or New
Year ritual in which her bearers challenge the householders to recite,
meeting verse with verse, or to open the door and let them partake of
the Christmas fare. A 'Wassail' ('be hale') is a similar ritual song (or
quête) usually from England. The one quoted here, however, is Phil
Tanner's from Gower and refers to a branch carried round and
decorated with ribbons by each household in turn. 'Souling' is also a
quête, but at Halloween. Children, representing the dead, sing and
beg for 'soul cakes.' The song I use comes from Hatterton on the
Cheshire-Shropshire border.

## ALL HALLOWS

It is your new year's day, the first
Of our winter, All Hallows,
When the quick darkening autumn
Swings ajar, and the ghosts come.


Like a dark stranger I knock.
Paul, I bring in my ignorance
The new year. Now, your whiteness
Open. We must give gifts and bless


To your further side of death
That glitters in the eclipse
So that one could almost swear
Light's bent from its corona,


And one sees for a second
The crowded windows, the good
Master and mistress within,
And welcome for our wassail . . .


No, there is no one. Threshold
Is dark, no one laughs or drinks.
But we with our Mari Lwyd
(That skeleton head of grief)


Call out: 'Answer if you can.
We bring the Great Queen's blessing.
Sing, answer us verse for verse
Or open to the Stranger.'


Silence. And we shuffle and wait,
And blame ourselves, our Mari
That is only a rotted skull
Of a mare in a grey sheet . . .

Silence.  And we for the want
Of any answer to silence
Praise raggedly our Goddess
And her gifts to the new dead.


'Our Mari is the world's rose,
The one blossom of winter.
On her broad white bone is gold,
Long lasting her scarred mantle.


And we are all St Mary's men,
And greet you for our lady
And for the sake of us all
Must offer Paul her presents.'


Silence.  Or was that a crack,
A key turning?  No, nothing.
I stumble out of our line
And lay on the stone four oakleaves.


'Since he had concern for earth,
For the land, for the holy
Terrain of Wales or Zion:
Since the soil, pebble or peat,


He made pictures from, Zion
Or Wales:  since the field of folk
Was first the deciduous field
Of the woods on Welsh uplands:


And since from the four-sided grave
Of Branwen by Llyn Alaw
He made a wildling garden
To echo the shape of Wales:

39

Now our Mari lays on the stone
For him, leaves brown and withered,
Oakleaves to be a covenant
Of our friendship with the land.'


Silence. I drop into line
Shy, ashamed of the tattered
Ins and outs of the dead leaves
And their dry-as-dust parchment.


'Answer if you can,' we sing,
'We bring the Great Queen's presents.'
And my billy comes forward
To lay rosehips on the stone.


'Since he'd concern for people,
For the knots that toil and bind,
For the unemployed—he lit
Their way home from Pride's office:


For the rubbished multitudes:
For the seed, the one lantern
Still lit on the mind's hillside:
For the well unpolluted:


Since he'd concern for the one
Who is what I am, human,
And since that one has suffered
In all who have ever died:


Now our Mari gives her own fruit
To him, rosehips red and swollen
Who is the world's rose, vials
Of blood for the seeds of time.'

'We are all St Mary's men,'
We sing, as a bright flicker
Of pride in our lady scuts
Across the drab lake of grief.


But no answer, no master
Or mistress of the dark hall
Unlatches the door for us . . .
A third steps down to the stone.


And this one lays down dark ivy,
Round leaves of an ivy bush
Umbelled with tiny blossom
Pricked from its peppercorn bud.


'Our Mari's gift, bitter gloss
Of immortality's ivy,
The evergreen survivor
Of the dead tree, image of art.


Our Mari's present,' he says,
And steps back without waiting
As the dark of All Hallows
Dies.  Look, on the horizon


The faint smudge of dawn.  Morning
Must not find us dressed like this.
The skull of grief's best hidden.
Wassail, wassail to you, Paul.

## ICON

We wake here. City. Hill.
Three crosstrees.
We wake into contours
Of what we do to each other.

We wake from our dream of reason.

We wake to a shape kneeling
Blue as distance.
'Ave,' it says. Little grey rectangles
Signify home. The platters of grace.

## HARVEST

It takes 10,000,000,000 years
In a universe
To talk to one another.
Words are like wheat on a slope.


By the silences we lie
Naked as leaves of wheat.
By the graven lakes, by the streams,
We root from the grain.

# MAPS (1)

for the wedding

No map can tell you all the ways—
What fences can be scraped through,
The white trespass to home,
All the heart's entrances.

True.  But you need trunk roads
To route you through long evasions.
You need the diversions marked
Round hold-ups and round bad temper.

*

Maps are all out of date
Before they are printed!

Still, as the arc of the night
Slices our crescent world,

As the ghost country through its legend
Usurps our rock—

You'll find Paul.
Verena is there.

# THE ELDBERRY BOUGH

Our Wassail is made of the eldberry bough,
He's the green man in the tree.
He's fun, he's a poet, he's in love.
He delves into glades gaudy with rubbish.

This is his tree.  Cartons, tins,
Coke bottles, all the confetti of time—
All the brides' polluted white
That trammels the dark.

Wassail, wassail, all rhymers sing,
Limners and dancers,
Those who blow, who pluck strings,
All who make, who bring Wassail—

*We know by the moon*
*        that we are not too soon*
*And we know by the sky*
*        that we are not too high.*

*We know by the stars*
*        that we are not too far*
*And we know by the ground*
*        that we are within sound.*

# MAP INTO HERALDRY

It is time to make shapes of my country.
Block them with hardboard,
Planks, bits and pieces.
Glue them, tack them down.

It is time we recognised that that shape
Had a future.
Make your templates brash
With the red and the gold.

It is time for the shape of Wales
To have a future.
Hoist it up with bravado
So the cock Wales can crow.

# BECCA AT THE GATE

You saw them shouting at Efail-Wen,
Preseli men round Mynachlog-ddu,
Swains of Llangolman and Maenclochog,
Farmhands, greybacks of Llandysilio—

You saw the wrath of Twm Carnabwth
The house-in-a-night man, who put stones
Round a hearth, a roof and a chimney
And a good fire alight by morning.

Gunfire and horsehooves in the darkness
And you saw Rebecca at the gate—
Red petticoats over ploughman's boots,
Bonnets and shawls, tall hats of women.

You were at the hosting at St Clears
Blackfaced on steeds round about Pwll Trap.
You saw the old bent Becca hobbling
Up to the gate, stooped on a thorn stick.

You saw the stick feel in front of her.
'Daughters, there's something put up here
Across the road, I cannot go on.'
Hundreds shouted, 'Mother, what is it?'

Nothing should bar your path, old Mother—
Not a great gate, nor bolted custom,
Nor opportunities taken away,
The theft that is wealth, or dumb respect.

You were with wassailers by moonlight
On familiar ground, under the stars.
Her cry rang out: 'Children, off with it,
Break the gate down, it's no business here.'

## MAPS (2)

When you first see one, the expressionist artwork
                                        engages you—
with colour,
with shape on its own terms,
a very modern crowding of disparate images
into design.


Then you see it is a map of Wales.


And that disappoints you.
You turn away from it as from impurity—


'I wish it was not so.'  Or, 'It is lesser
than it ought to be.'  Or even,


'He has sold out.'


                            *


But Wales is like perspective, it describes the space
imagination is using.  As in the inside-out
perspective of Chinese silks,
the vanishing point
is you.


After the twentieth map, you're part of the crowd.
Daughter of Becca, the gate's waiting.


You're faced with desolation and hope.

# SOULING

The high-pitched moaning song of soulers,
The primitive three-note wail of the dead—
Children traipsing the muddy roads
With the dead walking among them.

They cry for cakes. Dead and children
Cry. Or is it for a soul they sing
Or any good thing to make us merry—
Apple or pear, plum or cherry?

'A soul, a soul, a soul cake,
Pray, good missis, a soul cake'—
The wassail proper to this chink
Between seasons, All Hallows of the Dead.

And all our lives we cry for a soul
Through the brown lanes tripped by briar,
All our lives, and the stomach of death
Within us sings for its soul cake

Three thin notes of our banishment
From the hearth of the master and missis—
Tattered children and the wizened dead
In the hunger of the year.

'One for Peter, two for Paul,
Three for him who made us all'—
He who is three, the Rivals, traipsing
Through the dark with all that they have made.

# A BLOWN ALIBI

We wake from our dream of reason.
Uncertainty principles the light
That scars us, breaking
Like waves of half speech, a strange star.

The Maker in the yard of nothingness
Is dressed for his journey.
He does not see who else
Has a crown of thorns, a bloody back.

He puts on his papers.  His tree
Is shimmery with ribbons.
Carry it, it's a talisman,
It opens the gate.

He steps into the lane
And in procession the three thieves
Each with his tree
Walks down the scarring light.

But isn't there, at home, his ghost,
A surrogate man, washing up,
Putting the cat out,
An automaton?

So that if Seirian come
(His daughter) to ask
About homework,
He'll have time to be back,

A home for her, a father
Who does not have to appear
In the tatterjacket of papers
Or the grief of his tree.

He had time, in the twinkling of an eye,
To reassume the surrogate man
Before bedtime
And the harrowing of hell.

But that subterfuge is past.
The three trees
Are over the hill.
Darkness upon the world.

## WAS IT SO?

Maps were the wassail he took round.
He hawked them like a religion
From door to door, the lottery of faith.

'Will you sign?' Will you join this artwork—
Tie a knot here for the unemployed,
Come on board the Jubilee train?

His maps created an action committee, an affray.
We stood at Efail-wen before Thatcher
In our women's skirts, in the Falklands.

We were the very last unscheduled appearance of
Owain Glyndŵr. Not before time
We laid claim to the *bro* of summer stars.

# LYKE WAKE

But perhaps, in the crack of dreams,
He comes to your door.
He stands in the tattering air
Tagged with sorrow.

And you call from your bed,
Paul, is it you?
You rush to comfort him,
The hollow-eyed dead.

The papers rustle you away.
He's humble, he's seen hellfire.
He's on the Brig o' Dread.
He cries for a soul . . .

In the crack of dreams
Blue as distance
A shape kneels.  Gabriel
With the platters of grace.

## BABY TALK

And it is Christmas morning.


The innocent silver sea
Must learn to breathe,
Run on graven beaches,
Knuckle a cliff—


Must acknowledge the tricksy air,
The squirts of cloud.
Green hovers into fields.
Mist thins the world.


The Wales he made at Aber Alaw
In a rockgarden of wildlings
Climbs out of the night.


It is starry, it is Ephrath.


It is where Ann listened at Dolwar
To wassail of Methodists
On their wild travels.


It is Llanddewi-Brefi, a raised
Earth, a pulpit
For a blackbird or a saint.


It is Zion, it is clear water.
The wassailers come to drink.
An apple, a pear, a plum or a cherry,
Good master and missis, to make us merry.


And we sing by Paul's garden

'Witnesses, we bring wassail
　　To the Baby,
Wear the livery of his mother,
　　Our Grey Mari.


'In the manger he is helpless
　　(Spendthrift godhead
Bankrupt in a debtor's prison)
　　Our beloved!


'In your arms cutch all that's human
　　After travail,
You the world's rose and the mistress
　　Of our wassail.


'Through from slavery into freedom
　　Drives the fairway.
The whole world reborn All Hallows
　　For his birthday.'

# PROGRAMME NOTE

Though individual sections are given titles, they should not be read as separate poems.  The titles are a way of pointing the reader in the right direction, analogous to chapter headings.  Despite the efforts of concert programmes and the BBC over the years, there seems to be uncertainty about what a classical symphony involves:   so I have briefly indicated here the format of the first two movements.  The third is freer in structure, but based on the alternation of two main themes, the wassail and the map.  Please, though, ignore these notes if you don't find them helpful.

I.  The Shadow (sonata form).  For Raymond Garlick

| | |
|---|---|
| Collected Poems | slow introduction into |
| Choices | exposition lst theme, |
| Sanctity | bridge passage |
| Prologue in heaven | 2nd theme |
| Bus Stop | |
| Offering | |
| Homers | |
| Heroes | development |
| Over the top | |
| His family arrested | |
| Bill of lading | |
| All the fun of the fair | |
| Curriculum vitae | recapitulation, |
| Referendum | 1st theme |
| Belle View | |
| The Tree | 2nd theme |

II. Soldier (a Christmas scherzo) and Investiture (trio)

Soldier (part 1)

Shopping
Present
Stocking

Investiture, 1969

Soldier (part 2)

Party Games
Dressing up
Boxing day

III. All Hallows (A Wassail). For Paul Davies & Verena

All Hallows
Icon
Harvest
Maps (1)—for the Wedding
The Eldberry Bough
Map into Heraldry
Becca at the Gate
Maps (2)
Souling
A Blown Alibi
Was it so?
Lyke Wake
Baby Talk

Biographical Notes

Raymond Garlick
Paul Davies

# BIOGRAPHICAL NOTES

## RAYMOND GARLICK

Raymond Garlick came from England to university in Bangor. He was always a pacifist. He married a Welshwoman and became a Catholic and a Welsh nationalist committed to the formation of a bilingual Welsh state as part of Europe and the United Nations. He taught in Pembroke Dock, where he and Roland Mathias founded *Dock Leaves*, later *The Anglo-Welsh Review*, which he edited. He moved for a time to the slate-quarrying town of Blaenau Ffestiniog in Gwynedd; and then left Wales to teach in the Netherlands.

However, his children were growing up and he did not wish to deprive them of their Welsh birthright, so he came back to Wales in 1967, as a lecturer at Trinity College, Carmarthen. A year later Garlick's son became desperately ill. He tells us how 'I still come across sections of wall of which every detail, every irregularity, is minutely familiar; and realise that they are opposite bus stops where one stood . . . before hospital visits.' His son slowly and almost miraculously recovered, though his life had been despaired of.

In Garlick's absence in the Netherlands, Welsh resistance to anglicisation had stiffened. Cymdeithas yr Iaith Gymraeg (the Welsh Language Society) was mobilising Welsh youth into passive resistance and there were clashes with the police. His son was arrested, manhandled and beaten by the police, and imprisoned twice. His wife and sister-in-law also stood trial. His poems meditate on these matters: on the one side in the light of martyrdom—the Pope was at this time declaring several Welsh Elizabethan martyrs to be saints of the Church, a process to which Garlick gave his enthusiastic support; and on the other, in the conflict between Gandhi's pacifism and non-violent resistance and the sort of patriotic heroism represented by the sixth century Aneirin and the warriors of the Gododdin who rode from Edinburgh to try and retake Catraeth (now Catterick) from the English invaders.

The seventies, then, were a time of struggle, even of bewilderment for the poet; and they ended in disaster. His Welsh nationalism was hopelessly defeated in the St David's day 1979 Referendum on whether Wales should have a parliament; his marriage broke up; and his Catholicism was strained by the new reforms and the abandonment of Latin, and he slowly came to realise that he did not believe in the existence of a deity and never had, and that 'the whole thing had been make-believe—the response of the imagination to Latin Christianity as a superb art-form' (personal letter to the author). Since his retirement, however, he seems to have regrouped his resources and is now writing poetry again after a long silence.

For most of this information I am indebted to his autobiographical essay in *Artists in Wales 2*, edited by Meic Stephens (Gomer Press 1973) and to various articles and poems, and to personal communication.


## PAUL DAVIES

Paul Davies was born in Mumbles, Swansea, in 1947. His father was a vicar and he remained a committed Christian. He and his brother Peter both became artists. They founded Beca, or Becca in English (after the nineteenth century Rebecca riots against toll-gates), to provide a platform for radical and nationalist artists. Beca exhibitions were provocative events. They had names like Clymu a Chafflo (Knots and Tangles) where each visitor was invited to tie a knot in an enormous tangle of twine as a gesture of solidarity with the unemployed of Wales—each knot was supposed to represent one person out of work; or the last one before Paul died, Statws Swyddogol—Beca wrth y Glwyd (Official Status—Becca at the Gate). Paul's sympathy with poor people rubbished by Thatcherism was not just artistic. As a teacher and as a person he tried to give them confidence to be themselves.

He was a founder-lecturer of the Department of Art and Design in Gwynedd Technical College at Bangor. He was always starting projects, joining movements, agitating for art in Wales. As an artist he eagerly sought contacts all over Europe: his nationalism had no time for merely parochial vision. He tried to form broad fronts and support talent and initiative wherever he found it—though his support could be uncomfortable, restless and challenging. Like many visual artists he was often intellectually and verbally inaccurate, but unlike most painters he trusted words: he wanted to use them, to write manifestos, even to find a verbal equivalent for what his own art was doing. He used to come to me with some clotted bit of verbalism and I would try and sort out what he was saying into tolerable prose. There were times when I did not know what he wanted of me, and others when I felt he deferred to me too much. His sudden humility could be as deflating as his humour. He was determined I should be involved somehow or other with Beca—even as a poet with no very practical involvement in the visual arts. He would look at me quizzically sometimes and mutter, 'But of course you're visually illiterate, aren't you?'

Maps of Wales were certainly not his only format, though they probably dominated everything he did. He made them in two dimensions and in three— even in four, for his landscape maps, such as the one by the reservoir at Aber Alaw in Ynys Môn (near the four-sided grave of Branwen, the tragic heroine of Welsh legend) were made out of soil and stone, meant to change with weather and vegetation. He made maps in all sorts of media, expressive of many different feelings. Nor did he limit himself to Wales. The shape of the Holy Land claimed him as his religious apprehensions deepened; and one of his biggest projects—unfortunately never realised—was for a landscape map of the world to overlook Merthyr Tydfil.

Four of the sections of this movement of the poem were originally written for his wedding with Verena. They had two children, Seirian and Raffael.

61